Joint Coffee Campaign ad, 1922

19th century Turkish coffeehouse, Constantinople

COFFEE TIME

written by

Patrick Merrell and Helene Hovanec

interior design and illustration by

Patrick Merrell

Storey Publishing

*The mission of Storey Publishing is to serve our customers by
publishing practical information that encourages
personal independence in harmony with the environment.*

Edited by Lisa Hiley
Cover design by Tracy Johnson and Alethea Morrison
Cover illustration by Jon Cannell/Lilla Rogers Studio
Text Design by Patrick Merrell

Text © 2007 by Patrick Merrell and Helene Hovanec
Illustrations © 2007 by Patrick Merrell

Printed in the United States by CJK
10 9 8 7 6 5 4 3 2

 # Sit Back...

Is there any more effective antidote
to the everyday stresses of life than
a cup of hot coffee and a puzzle? Not
as far as we're concerned. We've
been hooked on both for more years
than you can shake a stirring stick
at...or a pencil, for that matter. And
we're not alone. People across the
globe have been savoring coffee
and enjoying puzzles for centuries.

In these pages, you'll find a bottomless cup of fun, fact, and fiction from the fascinating world of coffee blended with a mix of original word puzzles, sudoku, crosswords, brain teasers, word searches, acrostics, mazes, quizzes, and cryptograms.

So sit back, relax, and drink it all in, sip by delicious sip!

Patrick and Helene

World's
most popular
beverage:
water

World's
most traded
commodity:
oil

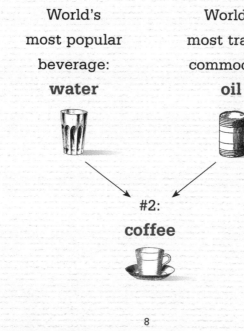

#2:

coffee

When I can't have my three daily demitasses of coffee, I'm as miserable as a dried-up piece of roast goat.

...

J. S. BACH and PICANDER
Coffee Cantata (1732)

*The very next thing
I'd like to do is smell
a cup of coffee.*

. . .

COMMANDER BILL McARTHUR
April 5, 2006, on the eve of returning to Earth after
six months aboard the International Space Station

On space missions, salt
and pepper come in liquid
form and coffee as a powder.

An astronaut's morning
"cupful" is rehydrated in a foil bag
and sucked through a straw.

Just Desserts

Look left, right, up, down, and diagonally both forward and backward to find 21 tasty treats that can be made with coffee.

BAKED ALASKA

BOMBE

BREAD

CAKE

FLAN

FLOAT

FUDGE

GELATO

GELÉE

GRANITA

ICE CREAM

ICING

MERINGUE

PIE

SAUCE

SORBET

SOUFFLÉ

SUNDAE

TART

TIRAMISU

TORTE

```
A T I N A R G N I C I
L K I C E C R E A M G
M D S N S O T A L E G
E Z T A O L F O B E R
N U U I L J E L R W E
T C G T R A T K A T T
E Y B N D A D Y A N E
B Y R N I A M E P C B
R Q U Z M R E I K X M
O S F U D G E R S A O
S O U F F L E M B U B
```

Just Desserts

NANCY ASTOR,
House of Commons member,
to her nemesis, Winston Churchill:

*If I were your wife
I would put poison
in your coffee!*

CHURCHILL:

*And if I were
your husband I
would drink it.*

COFFEE ON CURRENCY
Clockwise from top left: Haiti, Laos, Cameroon, Guatemala, Yemen, Uganda, Rwanda, Brazil, Congo, Colombia, and (center) Kenya

It's not unusual for coffee trees to display white flowers, green berries, and fully ripened red berries all at the same time.

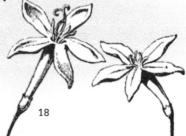

When the plantation flowered in the beginning of the rains, it was a radiant sight, like a cloud of chalk, in the mist and the drizzling rain.
...

ISAK DINESEN, *Out of Africa* (1937)

Groaners

ACROSS

1 Not on
4 Tape player
7 AWOL nabbers
10 Flower necklace
11 Shallow dishes
13 Snakelike fish
14 Shoe liners
15 **Irish coffee additives?**
17 Off the mark
19 Jr.'s son
21 Wild pigs
22 Curves
24 Furry flier
25 Accountant's book
26 **Southern helping of coffee?**
29 "Who am I?" condition
30 Strange
33 Patchwork clad plaything, often
34 Lace (up)
35 Family M.D.s
36 '60s G.I. tour
37 Stitch

DOWN

1 Charge chant
2 Charge
3 **Evaluations of brewing vessel buildups?**
4 Two-fingered gestures
5 Art able to
6 Hurry
7 **Superheated brewing vessels?**
8 Act as chairman
9 Draft org.
12 Make dove sounds
16 Old Mideast initials
17 Recede
18 Folded glove compartment item
20 Med. Sea borderer
22 "Just relax"
23 Univ. Web site ender
25 Girl rescued by Don Juan
27 Signed with a simple mark
28 "Help ___ the way!"
29 S.A. country
31 Cube with pips
32 Morning moisture

Groaners

O	F	F	■	V	C	R	■	M	P	S
L	E	I	■	S	A	U	C	E	R	S
E	E	L	■	I	N	S	O	L	E	S
■	■	M	U	G	S	H	O	T	S	■
E	R	R	A	N	T	■	■	I	I	I
B	O	A	R	S	■	B	E	N	D	S
B	A	T	■	■	L	E	D	G	E	R
■	D	I	X	I	E	C	U	P	■	■
A	M	N	E	S	I	A	■	O	D	D
R	A	G	D	O	L	L	■	T	I	E
G	P	S	■	N	A	M	■	S	E	W

The biggest coffee drinkers in the world?

Finns.

Finns consume about 30 pounds
of coffee per person per year. That's
around 1,200 cups a year for every
man, woman, and child in the country.

Legend has it that coffee was first discovered in Abyssinia, now Ethiopia, by a goatherd named Kaldi. One day, his goats began bleating and dancing about on their hind legs after eating the green leaves and red berries from an unusual tree. He tried some himself and was soon filled with an energy he thought would never end. Word spread and coffee quickly became an integral part of Ethopian life.

Instant History

500s: Coffee plants discovered in Ethiopia.

1500s: Exclusively cultivated in Yemen. Popular drink throughout the Ottoman Empire.

1600s: Coffee takes Europe by storm. India, Ceylon, and East Indies start growing it.

1700s: Coffee growing expands to Central and South America. American colonies adopt coffee as national beverage. History's only successful slave revolt takes place in Haiti, then source of over half the world's coffee.

1800s: Coffee growing escalates in Central and South America and expands to Hawaii.

1900s: Brazil leads the world in coffee exports. Popular drink in Japan after World War II.

Time-Out

Anagram each word and place it in the grid. Then read down the middle column for a "definition" of coffee.

BLEAT					
EAGER					
FLESH					
GATES					
KNEAD					
FREED					
LOANS					
SHRUB					
KNITS					
AIMED					

Speaking of Coffee

Anagram each word and place it in the grid. Then read down the middle column to find an answer to this riddle:

What language was the man speaking when he made coffee?

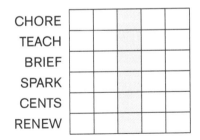

CHORE
TEACH
BRIEF
SPARK
CENTS
RENEW

Time-Out

T	A	B	L	E
A	G	R	E	E
S	H	E	L	F
S	T	A	G	E
N	A	K	E	D
D	E	F	E	R
S	A	L	O	N
B	R	U	S	H
S	T	I	N	K
M	E	D	I	A

BREAK
FLUID

Speaking of Coffee

O	C	H	E	R
C	H	E	A	T
F	I	B	E	R
P	A	R	K	S
S	C	E	N	T
N	E	W	E	R

HEBREW

Many people claim
coffee inspires them,
but, as everybody
knows, coffee only
makes boring people
even more boring.

...

HONORÉ DE BALZAC (1799–1850)

England's first coffeehouse opened in Oxford in 1650. Fifty years later, there were over 2,000 in London alone.

Right: Coffeehouses in London's Exchange Alley area prior to the fire of 1748. ● = Coffeehouse ◌ = Tavern

W.D. Woollen Drap[er]
Cook Eating House
Penfilvania Coffee House Richard
late Martin Notary
Marine Coffee H
Nicholas
Chapman

B I R C H I N - L A N E

CHURCH YARD

Wells
Emp. Wright
Wrapback Miller
Baynham
Fletcher Ins. Office
Horwick Leak Ford
Teyms
Huntingman
Cook Scots
Benfield
Salesheth Jan Rodan Male
Dicey's Cook

Sherman Cabinet
Miles Attorney
Hare Shop
Music Shop
Premier Shoe Maker
Gunpowder Office
Smith Butler
Cook Wigan
Trimerfby
Gary Smoaking Finest Razor
Glenn Parker
Swordblade Coffee H
Vinewater

Rainbow Coff Ho & Wilcock Books
Meadows Bookseller
M. Clean's Insurance Office
Fleece Trimmer
Jerusalem Coffee House
Wards Wagered Emmy Philpot Barber
Wilson Stationer
Richardson Colour Taylor

Fleece Passage
Brotherton Bookseller
Tom's Coffee House
Shipston
Deputy Cleeves Pewterer
Mrs Carter Milliner
Swan Passage
Strahan Bookseller
Warner Stationer
Swan Passage
Walthoe Bookseller
Astley Bookseller
Cotton & Lambert

Three Tuns, Roycroft
Swan Kitchen

EXCHANGE ALLEY

Darling Ins. Off.
Fred Elldrige Notary
Bartlett Ins Off.
Hogman

Richards Insurance Office Cancellor, Ins. Office
Watson Hatter
Peckover Watchmaker
Young Woollen Draper

Swan Barton
Jones and Horsley
Jonathan's Price

N L Haines English Ins Off
Homer Ins Off.

Garraway's
Wilson
Crown Alehouse
Langly Hatter
Blackwell Banker
South Seller
Bakers

Brooks Ins Off.
Sam's Coffee Ho.

'ARD - STREET
ABCHUR
Passage

Burnt
Damaged

E X C

Coffee leads men to trifle away their time, scald their chops, and spend their money, all for a little base, black, thick, nasty, bitter, stinking nauseous puddle water.

...

THE WOMENS PETITION
AGAINST COFFEE
London (1674)

THE MENS ANSWER TO THE
WOMENS PETITION AGAINST COFFEE
London (1674)

. . .

You may well permit us to talk abroud (sic), for at home we have scarce time to utter a word for the insufferable din of your active tongues.

Brewdoku

These nine letters fill the grid:

UMBER WALK

Each letter must appear once in each row, once in each column, and once in every 3x3 square.

The highlighted letters answer this clue:

Yoda's coffee
reheating instructions

R			U	E	B			K
		M	R					
		W			A	R	E	
M		L	K		R		U	W
K								L
U	A		M		W	K		E
	R	E	B			U		
					U	W		
L			W	K	M			R

Brewdoku

R	L	A	U	E	B	M	W	K
E	U	M	R	W	K	L	B	A
B	K	W	L	M	A	R	E	U
M	E	L	K	B	R	A	U	W
K	W	R	A	U	E	B	M	L
U	A	B	M	L	W	K	R	E
W	R	E	B	A	L	U	K	M
A	M	K	E	R	U	W	L	B
L	B	U	W	K	M	E	A	R

LUKEWARM or "LUKE, WARM"

The most expensive cans
of coffee in the world?

Andy Warhol's
"Martinson Coffee"
sold at auction for
$3,824,000 in 2006.

The silkscreen depicts 18 cans
of coffee. That's $212,444 per can!

In 1594, priests appealed to Pope Clement VIII to forbid Christians from drinking coffee, deeming it a "hellish black brew" created by Satan.

The Pope instead declared:

"Why, this Satan's drink is so delicious that it would be a pity to let the infidels have exclusive use of it. We shall cheat Satan by baptizing it."

Coffee Credits

When the credits roll at the end of movies and TV shows, they often include unnamed characters such as "man in bank" or "biker with beard." Hundreds have also included a reference to our favorite brown beverage:

> Man with Coffee
> Coffee Bouncer
> Coffee Chick
> Coffee Nurse
> Coffee Cake George
> Spilled Coffee Girl

Lucho, the Coffee Grower
Sasha, the Coffee Shop Dancer
Jerk in Coffee Shop
Annoying Coffee Patron
Coffee Drinker Under Window
Blurred Boy in Coffee Shop

Cold Coffee Lover
Veal Cutlet and Coffee Diner
Coffee Shop Cutie
Coffee Shop Bimbo
Coffee Gag Zombie
Coffee Shop Loser #3

Day Dream?

To find out the quip below, fill in the six
answers on the next page. Then transfer the
letters to the same-numbered spaces.

___
1

___ ___ ___ ___ ___ ___ ___
2   3   4   5   6   7   8

___ ___ ___ ___ ___ ___ ___
9 10 11 12 13 14 15

___ ___ ___ ___ ___ ___
16 17 18 19 20 21

___ ___ ___ ___ ___ ___
22 23   24 25 26 27

___ ___ ___ ___ ___.
28 29 30 31 32

1. 2005 Gwyneth Paltrow movie

‗‗ ‗‗ ‗‗ ‗‗ ‗‗
32   4   17   13   18

2. Seles of tennis fame

‗‗ ‗‗ ‗‗ ‗‗ ‗‗ ‗‗
2   3   7   22   16   1

3. Cutlery item

‗‗ ‗‗ ‗‗ ‗‗ ‗‗
26   5   10   19   30

4. Mean or erst follower

‗‗ ‗‗ ‗‗ ‗‗ ‗‗
9   12   25   29   27

5. Pretext

‗‗ ‗‗ ‗‗ ‗‗ ‗‗
8   14   6   28   31

6. Colonize

‗‗ ‗‗ ‗‗ ‗‗ ‗‗ ‗‗
23   20   11   15   24   21

Day Dream?

1. PROOF
2. MONICA
3. KNIFE
4. WHILE
5. GUISE
6. SETTLE

A MORNING WITHOUT
COFFEE IS LIKE SLEEP

*If I asked for a cup
of coffee, someone
would search for the
double meaning.*

...

MAE WEST (1892–1980)

Coffee Lingo

Coffee: java, joe, cup of joe, cuppa, cup of jolt, cupped lightning, battery acid, brew, daily grind, dope, draw one, drip, fluid, forty-four, forty weight, go juice, high octane, hot stuff, ink, jamoke, jet fuel, leaded, liquid lightning, mud, cup of mud, morning thunder, mother's little helper, paint remover, perky, rocket fuel, belly wash, blackout, black soup, black strap, creekbank, mouthwash, Brazil water

Black: no cow, barefoot, flowing Mississippi

Dark: with a splash

With milk: with socks on

Little milk: dry

Extra milk: wet

Milk and sugar: blonde and sweet, blonde with sand

With nonfat/low-fat milk: skinny

Decaffeinated: harmless, unleaded

With a shot of espresso: redeye, shot in the dark, scrap iron, speedball, depth charge, bellman, boilerhouse

Double shot of espresso: doppio

Two double shots: double-double, quad

To go: on a leash, with legs, travelin'

Decaf with nonfat milk: why bother?

Tasseography in the Middle East uses the sediment left in a cup of Turkish coffee to tell one's fortune.

*Coffee is hot
and dry and
very good for
the stomach.*

...

RHAZES, Persian physician
(850–922 A.D.)

The first written mention of coffee

Bean
Maze #1

Alternating between
roasted and unroasted
beans and moving only
one bean at a time either
left, right, up, or down
(not diagonally), find a
path from start
to end.

START

END

53

Bean Maze #1

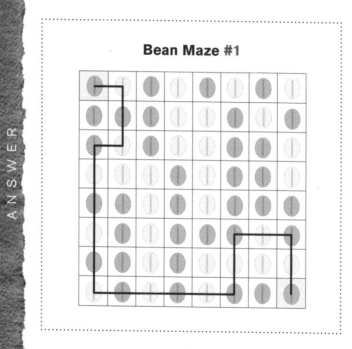

Coffee is a more powerful fluid than people generally think. A man in good health may drink two bottles of wine a day for a long time, and sustain his strength. If he drank that quantity of coffee he would become imbecile and die of consumption.

• • •

JEAN-ANTHELME BRILLAT-SAVARIN
The Physiology of Taste (1825)

Coffee should be black as hell, strong as death, and as sweet as love.

• • •

TURKISH PROVERB

In 17th century England, coffeehouses minted metal or gilded leather tokens for patrons to use because the government's coin supply was so small.

World's Largest Coffeepot... and Cup

Stanton, Iowa erected a unique tribute to hometown actress Virginia Christine, who played "Mrs. Olson" in Folgers Coffee commercials from 1965 to 1986. In 1971, the town converted its water tower into a gigantic coffeepot in her honor. A second tower shaped like a huge coffee cup, erected in 2000, won "Tank of the Year" from the Steel Plate Manufacturers Association.

THE POT: 125 feet tall with a capacity of 640,000 cups (40,000 gallons)
THE CUP: 96 feet tall with a capacity of 2,400,000 cups (150,000 gallons)

Work Ethic

One letter was inserted into each word below and the new words placed in the grid. Look for and circle the new words in all directions.

The added letters, reading from 1 to 19, will spell out the answer to this riddle:
Why did the waitress make so much coffee?

1. MOVE   I
2. MISER   ___
3. SELL   ___
4. MOUNT ___
5. INERT   ___

6. TINTS   ___
7. BEACH ___
8. HEATH ___

9. FLING   ___
10. PRICE   ___

11. ISLE   ___

12. CROWED   ___
13. COST   ___
14. EAST   ___'
15. HOTELS   ___

16. MOPED   ___
17. BACON   ___
18. STAND   ___
19. MONEY   ___

```
R V R M C C H L T F I
H T A M O U N T I S N
C M Z A O V L L E W S
A J S D D P I N Y R E
E T T M E N P E T L R
L H R J G D K E S P T
B E A C O N W I D R S
V A N D O Z A O Y I A
M L D M I S T E R N E
H T A I N T S Z H C Y
W H O S T E L S K E J
```

Work Ethic

```
R V R M C C H L T F I
H T A M O U N T I S N
C M Z A O V L L E W S
A J S D D P I N Y R E
E T T M E N P E T L R
L H R J G D K E S P T
B E A C O N W I D R S
V A N D O Z A O Y I A
M L D M I S T E R N E
H T A I N T S Z H C Y
W H O S T E L S K E J
```

IT WAS ALL IN A DAY'S PERK

1. I MOVIE
2. T MISTER
3. W SWELL
4. A AMOUNT
5. S INSERT
6. A TAINTS
7. L BLEACH
8. L HEALTH
9. I FILING
10. N PRINCE
11. A AISLE
12. D CROWDED
13. A COAST
14. Y YEAST
15. S HOSTELS
16. P MOPPED
17. E BEACON
18. R STRAND
19. K MONKEY

62

I believe that water is the only drink for a wise man; wine is not so noble a liquor; and think of dashing the hopes of a morning with a cup of warm coffee, or of an evening with a dish of tea! Ah, how low I fall when I am tempted by them!

. . .

HENRY DAVID THOREAU, *Walden* (1854)

Stereoscope card, 1900

11059—A Coffee-house in Palestine.

Although they be destitute of Taverns, yet have they their Coffa-houses, which something resemble them. There sit they chatting most of the day: and sippe of a drinke called Coffa in little China dishes, as hot as they can suffer it; blacke as soote, and tasting not much unlike it.

• • •

SIR GEORGE SANDYS, poet and traveler,
describing coffeehouses in Palestine and Egypt (1610)

The morning cup of coffee has an exhilaration about it which the cheering influence of the afternoon or evening cup of tea cannot be expected to reproduce.

...

OLIVER WENDELL HOLMES, SR. (1891)

In Jamaica,
bats sucking
on the ripe coffee
fruit at night is a
signal the beans
are ready to pick.

The Juan Valdez Quiz

Test your knowledge of the Colombian coffee icon.

1. Juan Valdez's faithful mule is named:
   A. Anita   B. Bambino   C. Conchita   D. Doritos

2. Juan Valdez had a cameo in what movie:
   A. *Bruce Almighty*   B. *Road to Rio*
   C. *Tea and Sympathy*   D. *Coffee, Tea or Me*

3. Juan Valdez represents cafeteros, which are:
   A. Coffee drinkers   B. Coffee actors
   C. Coffee growers   D. Cafeterias

4. Juan Valdez's portrayer:
   A. José F. Duval   B. Carlos Sánchez
   C. Carlos Castañeda   D. All of the above

Tube Test

How well do you know your television coffee-drinking spots? Match the TV show with the locale where the characters gather for a cup of brew.

1.____ *Frasier*   A. Monk's Cafe

2.____ *Friends*   B. Luke's Diner

3.____ *Seinfeld*   C. Central Perk

4.____ *Gilmore Girls*   D. Double R Diner

5.____ *Twin Peaks*   E. Cafe Nervosa

The Juan Valdez Quiz

1. C. Conchita.
2. A. *Bruce Almighty*. He poured a cup of coffee for Bruce, played by Jim Carrey.
3. C. Coffee growers.
4. D. All of the above. Duval, a New York-based actor, was the first, starting in1959. Sánchez, a Colombian coffee farmer, took over in1969. In 2006, Castañeda, a Andean coffee grower, became the third Juan.

Tube Test

1. E   2. C   3. A   4. B   5. D

*There are three intolerable
things in life—cold coffee,
lukewarm champagne,
and overexcited women.*

...

ORSON WELLES (1915–1985)

The
Percolator

The first percolator was invented in 1800 by Jean-Baptiste de Belloy, the Archbishop of Paris. Six years later, Count Rumford made considerable improvements and patented a design that looks a fair amount like modern models.

Rumford, born in Massachusetts as Benjamin Thompson, was a spy for the British who was forced to flee the colonies in 1776. He was eventually knighted by George III and then made a count of the Holy Roman Empire. He's also credited with inventing thermal underwear.

Left: De Belloy's drip pot
Right: Count Rumford's percolator

O Coffee!...This is the beverage of the friends of God...The intelligent man who empties these cups of foaming coffee, he alone knows truth...Coffee is our gold. Wherever it is served, one enjoys the society of the noblest and most generous men.

• • •

ARABIC POEM, "In Praise of Coffee" (1511)
from *The Maintenance of Purity as Regards the Legitimacy of Coffee*,
ABD-AL-KADIR (1587)

In the early 1900s, coffee trading in Yemen was conducted in an open-air exchange with buyers and sellers tapping finger codes into each others' palms. Handkerchiefs covered their hands to keep the bids secret.

Coffee Grinder

All the words in the list are made from the letters in COFFEE GRINDER. Place each one into the grid.

3 letters:

EGO

ERR

ONE

4 letters:

COIF   GRIN   REIN

CONE   ICON   RIFE

CORD   NICE   RING

5 letters:

CORGI   NIECE

DINER   OFFER

EDGER   REFER

FIEND   REIGN

6 letters:

CRINGE

IGNORE

REFINE

7 letters:

GREENER

NEEDIER

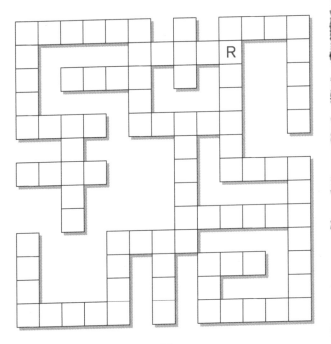

R

Coffee Grinder

Of all the unchristian beverages that ever passed my lips, Turkish coffee is the worst. The cup is small, it is smeared with grounds; the coffee is black, thick, unsavory of smell, and execrable in taste.

...

MARK TWAIN

The Innocents Abroad (1869)

To an old man, a cup of coffee is like the door post of an old house — it sustains and strengthens him.

...

OLD BOURBON PROVERB

The whirling dervishes of the Islamic Mevlevi Order achieve religious enlightenment by sharing a ceremonial red pot of coffee, then chanting to Allah and spinning in place for hours on end.

The original desktop image

Coffee Cam

The world's first live camera transmission on a computer network was of a coffee pot located in the old Computer Laboratory at the University of Cambridge. Set up in 1991, the image was updated several times a minute, allowing workers to check if the pot was full before making the trip for a refill.

The camera was connected to the Internet in 1993, allowing people around the world to keep track of the pot's status. And keep track they did. Over a million hits were recorded in 1996 and two years later that number had doubled.

When the camera was switched off in 2001, the pot was sold on eBay, with the proceeds of £3,350 going to fund coffee facilities in the university's new lab.

One Day at the Office

ACROSS

1 Oafs
6 Operated a car
11 Camera setting
12 Direct elsewhere
13 **Sign on the office vending machine one morning**
15 Invitation letters
16 Froth
19 Stanton residents (see page 58)
24 Barge's route
26 Mean
27 One who rates movies
29 Cowardly Lion portrayer
30 Animal fat
32 **Response that afternoon to the 13-Across sign**
39 "Take ___" (sit down)
40 Actress Witherspoon
41 Sharp twinges
42 Equally awful

DOWN

1 Fiscal exec.
2 Baton Rouge sch.
3 Baseball's Mel
4 "Welcome" site
5 Sunblock nos.
6 Let go of, from above
7 B'ball official
8 Switch setting
9 "Flying south" shape
10 Before, in poetry
14 Hot temperature, in old Rome
16 TV watchdog
17 Dinghy thingie
18 Indiana's capital?
20 Dances in triple time
21 Sly ___ fox
22 Ultimate degree
23 Isr. neighbor
25 ___ Hungarian rhapsodies
28 Unc's son or daughter
31 Poet Pound
32 Microwave, slangily
33 With 37-Down, a Gabor
34 Buddhist sect
35 Sharp turn
36 Grandpa Walton
37 See 33-Down
38 Last letter in London

One Day at the Office

C	L	O	D	S			D	R	O	V	E
F	S	T	O	P			R	E	F	E	R
O	U	T	O	F	C	O	F	F	E	E	
			R	S	V	P					
F	O	A	M			I	O	W	A	N	S
C	A	N	A	L			N	A	S	T	Y
C	R	I	T	I	C			L	A	H	R
				S	U	E	T				
Z	Z	Z	Z	Z	Z	Z	Z	Z	Z	Z	Z
A	S	E	A	T			R	E	E	S	E
P	A	N	G	S			A	S	B	A	D

Caffeine To Go

Looking for an extra buzz in the morning? "Coffee tights" contain microscopic capsules of caffeine that are activated by body heat. This, according to the Austrian manufacturer, increases the metabolic rate and burns fat in the thighs.

The tights, which cost about $18.00 a pair, must be worn every day for three weeks to achieve the best results, but unfortunately, the effects begin to weaken after five washings, presenting a struggle between slimmer thighs and personal hygiene.

I volunteered for the Union Army during the Civil War. Since I was just a teenager, one of my first assignments was to bring troops coffee and hot meals out on the front lines. Nobody on either side called time out — I could have been shot!

•••

PRESIDENT WILLIAM McKINLEY (1843–1901)

cof•fee (kô'fē) *n.*

The word coffee comes from the
Arabic *qahwa* through its Turkish
form, *qahveh*. Although coffee origi-
nated in or near Kaffa, in southwest
Ethiopia, there's no evidence that
the English word derives from this.
Interestingly, the Ethiopian word for
coffee is *bunc*, the only place in the
world where it isn't called something sounding like *coffee*.

Basque: *kaffia*

Bohemian: *kava*

Breton: *kafe*

Cambodian: *kafé*

Chinese: *kia-fey*

Croatian: *kava*

Czech: *káva*

Danish: *kaffee*

Dutch: *koffie*

Esperanto: *kafva*

Ethiopian: *bunc*

Finnish: *kahvi*

French: *café*

German: *kaffee*

Greek: *kaféo*

Hungarian: *kavé*

Italian: *caffè*

Japanese: *kéhi*

Latin: *coffea*

Persian: *qéhvé*

Polish: *kawa*

Portugese: *café*

Romanian: *cafea*

Russian: *kophe*

Serbian: *kafa*

Spanish: *café*

Swedish: *kaffee*

Turkish: *kahué*

Brew Ha Ha

Fill in the answers on the next page by combining syllables from the list below. The numbers in parentheses indicate the number of syllables in each answer. When you're done, the first and last letters of the answers, reading down, will reveal a "definition" of decaffeinated coffee.

AL	HAM	NESS	STEP
CO	IG	NO	THERE
EX	IN	PAIR	TRO
FORE	KI	RANT	TROUS
FRES	KI	RE	VERT
GOOD	MOCKS	SEAU	WAI

1. One way to dine (3) _____

2. Bride's stuff (2) _____

3. Uninformed (3) _____

4. "_____ gracious!" (2) _____

5. Outgoing person (3) _____

6. Fix (2) _____

7. Oahu beach (3) _____

8. Foot part (2) _____

9. Consequently (2) _____

10. Places for lazing (2) _____

Brew Ha Ha

1. ALFRESCO
2. TROUSSEAU
3. IGNORANT
4. GOODNESS
5. EXTROVERT
6. REPAIR
7. WAIKIKI
8. INSTEP
9. THEREFORE
10. HAMMOCKS

A TIGER WITHOUT STRIPES

*A supermarket is
where you spend
half an hour looking
for instant coffee.*

...

MAD MAGAZINE

*The government
of a nation is often
decided over a cup of
coffee, or the fate of
empires changed by
an extra bottle of
Johannisberg.*

. . .

G. P. R. JAMES
Richelieu (1829)

The Caffee Song

Carl Gottlieb Hering, born in Saxony in 1766, was a teacher and composer known for his children's songs. In this song, he changed the German spelling of *kaffee* to match the first six notes of the tune: C-A-F-F-E-E.

C-A-F-F-E-E,
    Don't drink so much coffee!
Not for children is the Turkish brew,
    Weakens the nerves, it's so bad for you,
Don't get hooked on the cup—
    One who can't give it up!

A raging tempest,
Tunisian pirates, and
a month of windless doldrums
didn't deter Frenchman Gabriel Mathieu
de Clieu from bringing a single coffee
plant from the garden of Louis XIV to
the island of Martinique in 1723. The
tree thrived in its new Caribbean setting and soon spread. The vast majority
of the coffee trees in the Americas today
are descendants of that one plant.

Pennies in a Mug

Fill a coffee mug just to the brim with water. If you gently slip a penny into the mug it won't overflow. How many more pennies do you think you could add before water spills out?

Dividing Mugs

Fourteen coffee mugs are on a table. Seven are filled with coffee and seven are half filled. Without changing the amount in any of the mugs, can you divide them into three groups so that each has the same total amount of coffee?

Pennies in a Mug

When we tried, we were able to add 60
pennies before it overflowed. Water has
a high surface tension and can bulge
upward quite a bit before its "skin"
breaks. Try it, and see how you do.

Dividing Mugs

Each row at
right adds
up to three
and a half
mugs of
coffee.

The world's most expensive coffee?

Kopi luwak, or civet coffee, can go for $300 a pound.

It's made by collecting undigested coffee beans from droppings of the palm civet, a small mongoose-like mammal of Southeast Asia.

Really.

IT IS CHEAPER TO BUY

ARBUCKLES'
ROASTED COFFEE

In One Pound Air-Tight Packages,

Than to Buy Green Coffee and Roast it yourself.

WHY?

Because four pounds of ARBUCKLES' ROASTED COFFEE will go as far as five pounds of green Coffee, as Coffee loses one-fifth in roasting by hand. Arbuckles' Roasted Coffee is much better, as every grain is evenly roasted, thus bringing out the full strength and aroma of the Coffee. You cannot roast Coffee properly yourself.

Left and above: An 1872 handbill for Arbuckles', America's first bagged coffee. In the Old West, Arbuckles' became synonymous with coffee.

Fair Trade

Though the dark days of slavery and indentured servitude in the coffee industry are past, many workers find themselves trapped in a life of poverty. By directly paying small, independent growers a fair price, fair trade wholesale buyers ensure that the workers earn a reasonable wage and can turn their hard work into a better life.

Shade-grown

Clear cutting forests and growing coffee in vast, open fields has been an increasing trend in recent years. This method requires large amounts of fertilizers and pesticides. By contrast, traditional shade farming allows coffee to grow under a natural tree canopy, maintaining and nurturing the local—and global—environment.

Gardening Tip

Look left, right, up, down, and diagonally,
both forward and backward. Circle each
word as you find it. Then read the leftover
letters to find a helpful gardening tip.

ACACIA	LILAC	PHLOX
ASTER	LILY	POINSETTIA
AZALEA	LOTUS	ROSE
CAMAS	NARCISSUS	SNOWDROP
CROCUS	OXALIS	SPIREA
FLAX	PEONY	SWEET WILLIAM
HEATHER	PERIWINKLE	TULIP
IRIS	PETUNIA	VIOLA

```
T U P O I N S E T T I A
S U E H E A T H E R E I
X A L F L C E S O R L C
N E O I F O F O I S K A
A L L E P A X P R N N C
R A C A M A S E I O I A
C Z L V L U U T S W W G
I A R I C O T U E D I N
S D S O L S O A S R R M
S U R L L Y L Y N O E P
U C C A I N U T E P P H
S W E E T W I L L I A M
```

Gardening Tip

USE COFFEE GROUNDS AS MULCH

Okay, we'll have coffee. Eh, how many lumps do you want?

...

BUGS BUNNY to PETE PUMA

before pulling out a huge wooden mallet

Rabbit's Kin (1952)

A crash in the coffee market directly preceded and helped bring about the 1929 stock market crash.

The Beatles made their debut on August 29, 1959, at the Casbah Coffee Club, a converted coal cellar in the basement of a Victorian house in Liverpool, England. George Harrison, Ken Brown, John Lennon, and Paul McCartney, known then as the Quarrymen, helped decorate the club before they played.

Frederick the Great vs. Coffee

In 1777, Frederick II, King of Prussia, issued a declaration: "It is disgusting to note the increase in the quantity of coffee used by my subjects . . . My people must drink beer. His Majesty was brought up on beer, and so were his officers . . . The King does not believe that coffee-drinking soldiers can be depended upon to endure hardships or to beat his enemies."

In spite of his official stance, Frederick himself indulged to the extreme, drinking "six or seven cups in the morning . . . and after lunch just one pot." And that was after cutting back. He once drank 40 cups of coffee to see if he could do without sleep, an experiment that so tortured his body that it was years before he considered himself fully recovered.

Brewdoku

These nine letters fill the grid:

CAKE HINTS

Each letter must appear once in each row, once in each column, and once in every 3x3 square.

The highlighted letters answer this clue:

**Place to find coffee…
or to find someone before
they've had their coffee**

H	C		E	S		N		A
S	T				A			I
		A			N		T	
A	S			K		I	N	
	H	C		A			S	E
	A		S			E		
C				A			H	T
N		K		T	H		A	C

Brewdoku

H	C	I	E	S	T	N	K	A
S	T	N	K	H	A	C	E	I
E	K	A	C	I	N	H	T	S
A	S	E	T	K	C	I	N	H
I	N	T	H	E	S	A	C	K
K	H	C	N	A	I	T	S	E
T	A	H	S	C	K	E	I	N
C	I	S	A	N	E	K	H	T
N	E	K	I	T	H	S	A	C

IN THE SACK

118

He was my cream,
and I was his coffee —
And when you poured
us together, it was
something.
...

JOSEPHINE BAKER
(1906–1975)

"Tip" is an acronym dating back to the old London coffeehouses, which put out brass boxes emblazoned with the inscription "To Insure Promptness" on them.

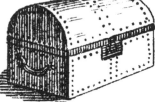

At breakfast we had a choice between tea and coffee for beverage; a choice not easy to make, the two were so surprisingly alike....As a matter of fact, I have seen passengers, after many sips, still doubting which had been supplied them.

• • •

ROBERT LOUIS STEVENSON
The Amateur Emigrant (1905)

A Cup of George

During World War I, the U.S. Army used a brand of instant coffee called George Washington's, with the result that doughboys often asked simply for "a cup of George."

A Cup of Joe

There are several theories as to the emergence of "joe" as a term for coffee: 1) from joe, a reference to the common man or a soldier; 2) the Stephen Foster song "Old Black Joe;" or 3) for Josephus Daniels, Wilson's Secretary of the Navy who abolished alcohol aboard ships. Coffee became the main alternative.

Just Joking

Put three of the letter groups together to form a nine-letter word that answers each clue. Write each word in the grid. The highlighted column will answer this riddle:

How did Abdul-Jabbar's teammates have their coffee?

AND	CKM	EST	IED	NAS	SOU
ATE	DIX	EWO	IEL	ONS	STI
BOY	EMB	FOR	IUM	POL	TER
CAM	END	FRI	LIF	QUA	THW
CHE	ERT	GYM	MAN	QUE	YES

1. Jury hotshot

2. Fit for the job

3. Grills

4. Arizona's region

5. Chess finale

6. Workout venue

7. Beau

8. Synthetic fabric

9. Jazz type

10. Soft cheese

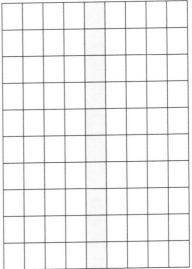

PUZZLE

Just Joking

F	O	R	E	W	O	M	A	N
Q	U	A	L	I	F	I	E	D
Q	U	E	S	T	I	O	N	S
S	O	U	T	H	W	E	S	T
C	H	E	C	K	M	A	T	E
G	Y	M	N	A	S	I	U	M
B	O	Y	F	R	I	E	N	D
P	O	L	Y	E	S	T	E	R
D	I	X	I	E	L	A	N	D
C	A	M	E	M	B	E	R	T

WITH KAREEM

40 percent of coffee drunk worldwide is instant. It's the #1 choice in Asia and accounts for 80 percent of the coffee consumed in the United Kingdom.

Coffee:
one who
is coughed
upon

I never knew a sailor, in my life, who would not prefer a pot of hot coffee or chocolate, on a cold night, to all the rum afloat.

• • •

RICHARD HENRY DANA, JR.
Two Years Before the Mast (1840)

Coffee Substitutes

Over the years, shortages, high prices, bans, and abstinence have given birth to a number of unusual coffee substitutes.

After England's Great Fire in 1666: betony root (mint family) and bocket, also known as saloop (a decoction of sassafras and sugar)

After Frederick the Great of Prussia made coffee an expensive state monopoly in 1781: barley, wheat, corn, chicory, and dried figs

From General Sherman's Civil War memoirs:
Indian corn, sweet potato, and okra seeds

Fruit: dates, juniper berries, cranberries, holly berries, sloes, orange peel, and cherry pits

Seeds: hemp, pumpkins, gherkins, sunflowers, limes, chrysanthemums, cotton, and gorse

Nuts: roasted acorns, almonds, and peanuts

And the list goes on: artichokes, asparagus, carrots, parsnips, dandelions, dahlia tubers, beetroots, rice, malt, lupins, chick peas, carob beans, reeds, molasses, cane, bracken, burrs, vetch, cacao husks, and wine dregs

CBers

Like "coffee break," each of these answers has the initials "CB." Use the clues to fill in each answer, then read down the highlighted letters to find a "definition" for a coffee break.

1. Mythological archer's "love weapon"
2. Crayons are used to fill in its pages
3. Surface for chopping vegetables
4. Snickers or 3 Musketeers

5. Big firecracker with a fruity name
6. Cardboard container filled with Life
7. Liquid often used to make soup
8. White one on a pool table
9. Old West footwear (plural)
10. Auto's electricity source

1. C _ _ _ _ ' _ B _ _

2. C _ _ _ _ _ _ _ B _ _ _

3. C _ _ _ _ _ _ B _ _ _ _

4. C _ _ _ _ B _ _

5. C _ _ _ _ _ B _ _ _

6. C _ _ _ _ _ B _ _

7. C _ _ _ _ _ _ B _ _ _ _

8. C _ _ B _ _ _ _

9. C _ _ _ _ _ B _ _ _ _

10. C _ _ B _ _ _ _ _

CBers

CUPID'S BOW
COLORING BOOK
CUTTING BOARD
CANDY BAR

CHERRY BOMB
CEREAL BOX
CHICKEN BROTH
CUE BALL
COWBOY BOOTS
CAR BATTERY

POUR EXCUSE

134

The term "coffee break" was coined in 1952 by the Pan American Coffee Bureau in a series of ads featuring the slogan:

Give yourself a coffee break... and get what coffee gives to you!

Last comes the beverage of the Orient shore,
Mocha, far off, the fragrant berries bore.
Taste the dark fluid with a dainty lip,
Digestion waits on pleasure as you sip.

• • •

POPE LEO XIII, "Frugality" (1898)
written at the age of 88

The Colombian National Coffee Park in Montenegro offers traditional theme park rides, as well as a coffee museum, food stands with coffee products, an ecological walk through a coffee grove, a re-creation of a native cemetery, and a bihourly show featuring 120 mechanical orchids that sing and dance.

Patrons of 17th century London coffeehouses could hear lectures on astronomy, mathematics, chemistry, and "experimental philosophy," which included mechanics, pneumatics, optics, and hydrostatics.

Coffee when well prepared is beyond question one of the ambrosial luxuries of modern life.

...

WILLIAM M. LESZYNSKY, M.D.
Coffee as a Beverage (1901)

Fact Simile

Fill in the eight answers on the next page. Then transfer the letters to the same-numbered spaces below to find a poetic description of a brewed beverage.

$\overline{}_{1}$ $\quad$ $\overline{}_{2}$ $\overline{}_{3}$ $\overline{}_{4}$ $\overline{}_{5}$ $\quad$ $\overline{}_{6}$ $\overline{}_{7}$

$\overline{}_{8}$ $\overline{}_{9}$ $\overline{}_{10}$ $\overline{}_{11}$ $\overline{}_{12}$ $\overline{}_{13}$

$\overline{}_{14}$ $\overline{}_{15}$ $\overline{}_{16}$ $\overline{}_{17}$ $\overline{}_{18}$ $\quad$ $\overline{}_{19}$ $\overline{}_{20}$ $\quad$ $\overline{}_{21}$

$\overline{}_{22}$ $\overline{}_{23}$ $\overline{}_{24}$ $\overline{}_{25}$ $\overline{}_{26}$ $\overline{}_{27}$ $\overline{}_{28}$ $\overline{}_{29}$

$\overline{}_{30}$ $\overline{}_{31}$ $\overline{}_{32}$ $\overline{}_{33}$ $\overline{}_{34}$

1. Put stuff in folders

    ―― ―― ―― ――
    11   1   15 27

2. Use your brain

    ―― ―― ―― ―― ――
    34 33   3 25 18

3. Hawaiian coffee area

    ―― ―― ―― ――
    4 23 30 19

4. Small movie role

    ―― ―― ―― ―― ――
    17 21   6 12 24

5. Scale (a mountain)

    ―― ―― ―― ―― ――
    8 26 31 22 14

6. Dentist's advice

    ―― ―― ―― ―― ――
    10   2   9 20 29

7. Petrol

    ―― ―― ――
    32 16 28

8. Ophthalmologist's concern ―― ―― ――
    5   7 13

PUZZLE

141

Fact Simile

1. FILE
2. THINK
3. KONA
4. CAMEO
5. CLIMB
6. FLOSS
7. GAS
8. EYE

I LIKE MY COFFEE BLACK
AS A MOONLESS NIGHT

Suave molecules of Mocha stir up your blood...the organ of thought receives from it a feeling of sympathy. ...

PRINCE TALLEYRAND (1754–1839)

NASA's solar-powered
Pathfinder Plus UAV

NASA & Coffee

In 2002, NASA's Uninhabited Aerial Vehicle (UAV) Coffee Project had a remotely piloted, solar-powered airplane cruising over and taking digital pictures of Hawaii's largest coffee plantation. By analyzing the color patterns in the images, researchers on the ground could quickly determine which fields were ready for machine harvesting.

Although a valuable eye in the sky for coffee growers or other farmers, the ultimate goal of the project was to develop imaging technology that could be used for weather observation, communications, agriculture, disaster monitoring, and emergency response.

The powers of a man's mind are directly proportioned to the quantity of coffee he drinks.

...

SIR JAMES MACKINTOSH (1765–1832)

From the 1902 Sears, Roebuck Catalogue

No. 7R117 For $2.10 we will furnish 10 pounds of this our own special grade of roasted coffee, complete with large enameled covered 10-pound tin canister. Price for 10-pound can.. ....$2.10

No. 7R118 For $1.10 we will furnish 5 lbs. of this our own special grade of roasted coffee, complete with large enameled covered 5-lb. tin canister. Price... ....$1.10

Our 20-Cent Side Coffee Mill.

No. 23R922 Side Mill, hardwood board, polished and varnished, iron japanned, medium size.

Price, each.........20c

This Coffee Tastes Like...

ACROSS

1 European mountain
4 CPR giver, perhaps
7 "Errr..."
10 "Could be"
12 Prefix with classic
13 **With 33-Across, explanation as to why the coffee tasted like 19-Down**
15 Loch ___ monster
16 White stickum
17 Not "Away" athletes
20 Mauna ___ volcano
23 Sound abbr.
24 Librarian's deg.
25 One who might pull an upset
28 Tennis's Monica
29 Japan's locale
33 **See 13-Across**
36 Chest bone
37 Last part of a chess match
38 UFO drivers
39 Denials
40 Club ___ resort

DOWN

1 Not fer
2 Pear-shaped instrument
3 Church benches
4 Double curve
5 Chinese food additive
6 Sub weapon
7 Sitting idle
8 ___ telepathy
9 Web surfers' needs
11 MISS USA is written on it
14 Horse tidbit
18 Rowers
19 **See 13-Across**
20 Brilliance, to a Brit
21 Flash-in-the-pan singer's claim
22 Improvised jokes
26 Some M.I.T. grads
27 Group of toughs
30 Thailand, once
31 "By the power vested ___..."
32 Got older
34 Lennon's wife
35 Sts.

PUZZLE

This Coffee Tastes Like...

A	L	P	■	E	M	T	■	U	M	M
G	U	E	S	S	S	O	■	N	E	O
I	T	W	A	S	G	R	O	U	N	D
N	E	S	S	■	■	P	A	S	T	E
■	■	■	H	O	M	E	T	E	A	M
L	O	A	■	A	U	D	■	D	L	S
U	N	D	E	R	D	O	G	■	■	■
S	E	L	E	S	■	■	A	S	I	A
T	H	I	S	M	O	R	N	I	N	G
R	I	B	■	E	N	D	G	A	M	E
E	T	S	■	N	O	S	■	M	E	D

A mortar and pestle for grinding coffee was among the cargo aboard the *Mayflower*.

Mortar and pestle belonging to the parents of Peregrine White, the first English child born in the New World

You can tell when you have crossed the frontier into Germany because of the badness of the coffee.

...

EDWARD VII (1841–1910)

Although a coffee tree can continue blooming for 50 years, the best crops come between the fifth and fifteenth years.

S. Thomassin Sculp.

BRAVE, clean, lithe, sturdy fellows, they were. Clear of eye, steady of nerve, strong of heart,—splendid physical specimens. "The finest soldiers in the world",—has been said of them. And they *proved* it!

Coffee lovers, they were—almost to a man. Coffee drinking had been their habit all their lives. They were practically raised on it, in the true American fashion. And they were not *deprived* of it!

A most careful diet was planned in order to maintain health and strength. While bread and beans and beef were needful, there was one item recognized as absolutely indispensable—*coffee*.

So—whatever else they had, our boys had their coffee,— plenty of it, *four times a day!* It cheered and comforted and encouraged them. It helped them do their job,—and do it well. Who shall say how *grand* a part coffee played in this great war?

Coffee— *the Essential drink*

Family Ties

In this substitution code, one letter stands for another. Start with the hint and use logic and your familiarity with short words to decipher the quip.

Hint: Q = T

YUQJTVA XVT VTXHHZ

ASTENXH RTEXFAT QJTZ

EXP ITQ FS NP QJT

YUVPNI RTKUVT QJT

AYTHH UK EUKKTT.

Commander-in-"Chef"

Here's another substitution code
using a different set of swapped letters.

Hint: B = S

U W O K M K B O U W P L F I O N U S

F A N H O R M K B U S K W O H E X B B K B

B. P M F W O: "V K N L O K W Q F S K

V U B K W O U M K Q K F E H R N W F

B E U I K S I H I H Q A K M F W S F

I H R N L I N L L K K."

ANSWER

Family Ties

Mothers are really special because
they can get up in the morning
before the smell of coffee.

Commander-in-"Chef"

Interesting factoid about President
Ulysses S. Grant: "He often made
his entire meal upon a sliced
cucumber and a cup of coffee."

Coffeehouse chess

can be both good and bad. Chess clubs use the term to describe their play as fresh, fun, and spirited. "Serious" players more often use it to describe amateur play that relies on cheap tricks, wild attacks, or cheating.

Reversible
Coffee

The halfway point of this book
seems like a fitting spot for this
ambigram, a typographic design
that reads exactly the same
when rotated 180 degrees.

I believe I forgot to tell you one Anecdote: When I first came to this House it was late in the Afternoon, and I had ridden 35 miles at least. "Madam" said I to Mrs. Huston, "is it lawfull for a weary Traveller to refresh himself with a Dish of Tea provided it has been honestly smuggled, or paid no Duties?"

"No sir, said she, we have renounced all Tea in this Place. I can't make Tea, but I'll make you Coffee." Accordingly I have drank Coffee every Afternoon since, and have borne it very well.

Tea must be universally renounced. I must be weaned, and the sooner, the better.

. . .

JOHN ADAMS IN A P.S. TO HIS WIFE (July 6, 1774)

Bean
Maze #2

Alternating between
roasted and unroasted
beans and moving
diagonally only one
bean at a time, find
a path from start
to end.

START

END

165

Bean Maze #2

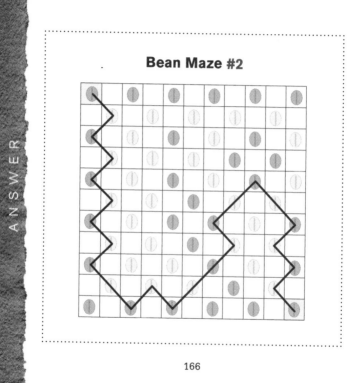

166

Coffee:
(acronym)
Come
over for
free energy
everyday

"Coffee and..."

Many songs have been written about coffee, including these whose titles start with the words: COFFEE AND...

A BAGEL
BEANS
BRANDY
CAKES
CANDLES
CIGARETTES
CIGS
CREAM

KISSES
MARGARITAS
ME
NICOTINE
ORANGES
PRAYERS
TEA
THE BIBLE

Well, one can die after all; it is but dying; and in the next world, thank God, there is no drinking of coffee and consequently no waiting for it.

...

IMMANUEL KANT (1724–1804)

A popular Arab legend tells of a sheik named Omar who was driven into the desert by his enemies in the year 1258. Facing starvation, Omar ate the berries of a strange tree, eventually roasting and soaking them to lessen the bitter taste. The brown liquid helped sustain him and when he returned to Mocha, his salvation was considered a miracle. News of the berries spread and Omar was made a saint.

Fund Raiser

One letter was removed from each word below
(without rearranging the remaining letters)
and the new words placed in the grid. Look
for and circle the new words in all directions.

The removed letters, reading
from 1 to 13, will spell out the name
of an informal political fund raiser.

1. CREEK   C
2. SALOONS   ___
3. REFUSES   ___
4. RIFLE   ___
5. FEATHERS   ___
6. SCALED   ___

7. SMOOTHED ___
8. FORAY   ___
9. FRACTION   ___
10. CONVERT   ___
11. DIETER   ___
12. BLINTZ   ___
13. TIGER   ___

```
T H D L A C S S
E L I R O Z C N
S S W V E T O O
O F E B D I L L
O R F S T L T A
T A R C U B T S
H Y A Z (K E E R)
E F A T H E R S
D E T E R Q Z B
```

173

Fund Raiser

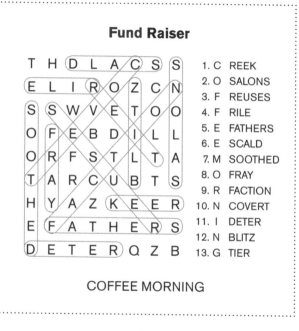

1. C	REEK
2. O	SALONS
3. F	REUSES
4. F	RILE
5. E	FATHERS
6. E	SCALD
7. M	SOOTHED
8. O	FRAY
9. R	FACTION
10. N	COVERT
11. I	DETER
12. N	BLITZ
13. G	TIER

COFFEE MORNING

174

During the Civil War, the Union Army used an early form of instant coffee: a thick, gooey paste made of ground coffee, sugar, and milk. All a soldier had to do was open the can and add hot water.

I think it must be slow. I've been drinking it for eighty-five years and I'm not dead yet!

...

FONTENELLE (1657–1757)
after being told coffee was "slow poison"
(Also attributed to Voltaire, although he died at 84)

176

Jean-Paul Sartre is sitting in a French café revising his draft of *Being and Nothingness*.

He says to the waitress, "I'd like a cup of coffee, please, no cream."

The waitress replies, "I'm sorry, monsieur, but we have no cream, only milk."

"Make it no milk then."

Early 1900s

Let me make my Husband's coffee — and
*   I care not who makes eyes at him!*
Give me two matches a day—
One to start the coffee with, at breakfast,
*   and one for his cigar, after dinner!*
And I defy all the houris in Christendom to
*   light a new flame in his heart!*

• • •

HELEN ROWLAND
"What Every Wife Knows"

Late 1900s

· · ·

FEMINIST POLITICAL BUTTON

Brewdoku

These nine letters fill the grid:

SHAKY WIRE

Each letter must appear once in each row, once
in each column, and once in every 3x3 square.

The highlighted letters answer this clue:

**Drink containing all
four major food groups:
Coffee with cream, sugar, and _____**

	R						W	
Y			K	H	R			I
		E				R		
W		A	E		S	Y		R
			A		I			
E		Y	W		H	I		S
		K				H		
I			S	W	K			A
	A						S	

181

Brewdoku

K	R	I	Y	E	A	S	W	H
Y	W	S	K	H	R	A	E	I
A	H	E	I	S	W	R	Y	K
W	I	A	E	K	S	Y	H	R
H	S	R	A	Y	I	W	K	E
E	K	Y	W	R	H	I	A	S
S	E	K	R	A	Y	H	I	W
I	Y	H	S	W	K	E	R	A
R	A	W	H	I	E	K	S	Y

WHISKEY

Perhaps the most vicious anti-coffee campaign was during the Ottoman reign of Murad IV. The Grand Vizier Kuprili not only banned coffee but ordered cudgeling and imprisonment for the first offense. Second offenders were sewn in a leather bag and thrown in the Bosphorus.

The Top 5 Coffee Importers

1 UNITED STATES
2 GERMANY
3 ITALY
4 JAPAN
5 FRANCE

Behind the numbers: The U.S. accounts for 25 percent of all imports. Germany's total is 10 percent, although half of that is reexported, mostly to Eastern European countries. Japan actually surpasses Italy in consumption since Italy reexports about 25 percent of its coffee.

The Top 5 Coffee Exporters

1 BRAZIL
2 VIETNAM
3 COLOMBIA
4 GERMANY
5 INDONESIA

Behind the numbers: Brazil accounts for about one-third of exported coffee. In recent years, Vietnam has grown into a major producer of coffee, although most of it is of the cheaper robusta variety. Germany is a surprising #4 since it grows no coffee itself (see *Importers*).

If you like your coffee with sand for dregs,
A decided hint of salt in your tea,
And a fishy taste in the very eggs —
By all means choose the Sea.

. . .

LEWIS CARROLL, "A Sea Dirge" (1861)

In Middle Eastern homes, guests are often welcomed with a traditional coffee ceremony.

A pan of green beans is roasted in a flat, open pan for all to smell. They're cooled on a small straw mat and then ground using a large mortar and pestle. The coffee is brewed in a traditional clay pot and served in small cups.

The ritual is as much about enjoying the process and the coffee as it is each others' company.

Excuses, Excuses

Fill in the missing letters to answer the clues. Then read the filled-in letters (left to right, top to bottom) to find a coffee lover's excuse for tardiness.

Clue	Answer
Uprises	R E __ __ L S
Small	L I __ __ L E
Type of bar	E N __ __ G Y
Buckingham, e.g.	P A __ __ C E
Needle work?	T A __ __ O O
Frost's field	P O __ __ R Y
Cornell's home	I T __ __ C A
Victor	W I __ __ E R
Football team	E L __ __ E N
Veer	S W __ __ V E

Three-for-All

Place a three-letter group from the box on each line to form an ordinary word. Then read the filled-in letters to find a quip.

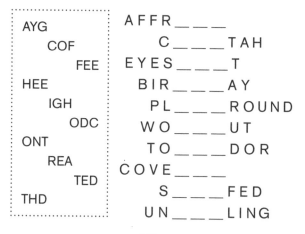

AYG
COF
FEE
HEE
IGH
ODC
ONT
REA
TED
THD

A F F R _ _ _
 C _ _ _ T A H
E Y E S _ _ _ T
 B I R _ _ _ A Y
 P L _ _ _ R O U N D
 W O _ _ _ U T
 T O _ _ _ D O R
C O V E _ _ _
 S _ _ _ F E D
 U N _ _ _ L I N G

P U Z Z L E

Excuses, Excuses

REBELS
LITTLE
ENERGY
PALACE
TATTOO
POETRY
ITHACA
WINNER
ELEVEN
SWERVE

BETTER LATTE
THAN NEVER

Three-for-All

AFFRONT
CHEETAH
EYESIGHT
BIRTHDAY
PLAYGROUND
WOODCUT
TOREADOR
COVETED
SCOFFED
UNFEELING

ON THE EIGHTH
DAY GOD
CREATED COFFEE

O plant, given to the human race by the gift of the Gods!

No other out of the entire list of plants has ever vied with you.

On your account sailors sail from our shores and fearlessly conquer the threatening winds, sandbanks and dreadful rocks.

. . .

GUILLAUME MASSIEU
"Caffaeum" (1718)

In 1907, while staying at the renowned Maxwell House Hotel in Nashville, TN, President Teddy Roosevelt raved that the house blend was "good to the last drop." The Cheek-Neal Coffee Company, which supplied the hotel with the special blend, soon adopted the phrase, making Teddy Roosevelt perhaps the only president to also be an advertising slogan writer.

*I never drink coffee
at lunch. I find it
keeps me awake for
the afternoon.*

...

reputedly by RONALD REAGAN (1980s)

THE

WHITE·HOUSE
COOK·BOOK

COOKING, TOILET AND HOUSEHOLD RECIPES,

MENUS, DINNER-GIVING, TABLE ETIQUETTE,

CARE OF THE SICK, HEALTH SUGGESTIONS,

FACTS WORTH KNOWING, Etc., Etc.

THE WHOLE COMPRISING

A COMPREHENSIVE CYCLOPEDIA OF INFORMATION FOR THE HOME

1887 best-seller by Mrs. Fanny Gillette (of razor family fame)

WHITE HOUSE COFFEE

One full coffee cupful of ground coffee, stirred with one egg and part of the shell, adding a half cupful of cold water. Put it into the coffee boiler and pour on to it a quart of boiling water; as it rises and begins to boil, stir it down with a silver spoon or fork. Boil hard for ten or twelve minutes. Remove from the fire and pour out a cupful of coffee, then pour back into the coffeepot. Place it on the back of the stove or range where it will keep hot (and not boil); it will settle in about five minutes.

Half a Mug

One coffee mug is empty. The other, of
a different size and shape, is filled to the brim.
Using only the mugs, how can you pour exactly
half from the filled mug to the empty one?

A Finger in the Mug

Two mugs filled with coffee are balanced on a scale. If you dipped your finger halfway into the coffee on the right (don't worry, it's cold), would that side go up, down, or stay the same?

Half a Mug

Looking directly from the side, the interior
of the filled mug is a rectangle. Slowly
pour the coffee out until the liquid
remaining in it forms a diagonal
line from the mug's lip to the
opposite, bottom corner. That
will be exactly half the volume.

A Finger in the Mug

The right side will be heavier and will go
down. Your finger displaces an amount
of coffee equal to the size and weight of
your finger, increasing the mug's weight.

In Dieppe, France, it's customary to toast weddings and baptisms with coffee rather than wine.

For lo! the Board with Cups
  and Spoons is crown'd,
The Berries crackle, and
  the Mill turns round;

On shining Altars of Japan they raise
The silver Lamp; the fiery Spirits blaze:
From silver Spouts the grateful Liquors glide,
While China's earth receives the smoking Tyde:
At once they gratify their Scent and Taste,
While frequent cups prolong the rich Repast;
Strait hover round the Fair her Airy Band;
Some, as she sipp'd, the fuming Liquor fann'd,
Some o'er her Lap their careful Plumes display'd,
Trembling, and conscious of the rich Brocade.

Coffee, (which makes the Politician wise,
And see thro' all things with his half-shut Eyes)
Sent up in Vapours to the Baron's brain
New Stratagems, the radiant Lock to gain.
Ah cease rash Youth! desist ere 'tis too late,
Fear the just Gods, and think of Scylla's fate!
Chang'd to a Bird, and sent to flit in Air,
She dearly pays for Nisus' injur'd Hair!

• • •

ALEXANDER POPE
"Rape of the Lock," Canto III (1714)

Berries crackle: coffee beans crackle
Altars of Japan: tables coated with a Japanese tree varnish
China's...Tyde: China cups receive the steaming coffee

Caffeine Content

Preparation methods vary, as do brands,
but here are comparative amounts in mg
for **ONE OUNCE** of…

Decaf coffee	0.6
Hot cocoa	0.6
Cola	3.5
Green tea	3.75
High caffeine soda	4.6
Black tea	6
Instant coffee	12
Brewed coffee	17
Espresso	40 and up

A freak "black frost"
that hit Brazil in
1975 killed well over
half its coffee plants.
That's one and a half
billion trees!

Tongue Twister
Coffee Grams

Change each verbose sentence into a four-word sentence where all the initial letters are the same. Write the answer on the line below each sentence.

Example:

Perhaps people in the upper echelons of corporations will prepare a coffee-chocolate beverage =
MANAGEMENT MIGHT MAKE MOCHA

1. Is it possible that President Eisenhower insisted on having an "unleaded" beverage?

_____

2. Adorable food preparation experts lust after a frothy drink.

_____

3. Trained coffee preparers from a large South American country are quite inferior at tooting their own horn.

---

4. Strikingly strange residents of Cairo and Luxor have an affinity for a strong brewed beverage.

---

5. The ingestion of the most prevalent substance in coffee neutralizes insanity.

---

6. The scents of non-robusta seeds excite octogenarians and others of their ilk.

---

7. I suggest that we depart from a nation obsessed by a steamed milk drink.

---

8. Imbibers who live in Saharan regions are entitled to end-of-meal treats.

Tongue Twister Coffee Grams

1. Did Dwight demand decaf?
2. Cute cooks (chefs) crave cappuccino.
3. Brazilian baristas boast (brag) badly.
4. Exotic (eerie) Egyptians enjoy espresso.
5. Caffeine consumption counteracts (cures) craziness.
6. Arabica aromas arouse ancients.
7. Let's leave latte land.
8. Desert drinkers deserve desserts.

Congratulations if you came up with alternates.

Joint Coffee Campaign ad, 1922

Serve
COFFEE
when you entertain

An abridged version of

To the Coffee House!

PETER ALTENBERG, Vienna poet (1859–1919)

When you are worried, have trouble of one sort
or another — to the coffee house!
When she did not keep her appointment, for
one reason or other — to the coffee house!...
When your income is four hundred crowns
and you spend five hundred — coffee house!
You are a chair warmer in some office, while
your ambition led you to seek professional
honors — coffee house!...
You hate and despise human beings, and at
the same time you can not be happy
without them — coffee house!

You compose a poem which you can not inflict upon
*   friends you meet in the street — coffee house!*
When your coal scuttle is empty, and your gas
*   ration exhausted — coffee house!*
When you need money for cigarettes, you touch
*   the head waiter in the — coffee house!...*
When you acquire a new flame, and intend
*   provoking the old one, you take the new one*
*   to the old one's — coffee house!*
When you feel like hiding you dive into a —
*   coffee house!*
When you want to be seen in
*   a new suit — coffee house!*
When you can not get
*   anything on trust*
*   anywhere else*
*   — coffee house!*

Cherries...

The fruit of the coffee tree is called a cherry because it is bright red when ripe. The cherries grow clustered down the length of a branch, taking six months to turn from green to yellow to red.

...and Beans

The seeds of the coffee plant, or beans, look like tiny, green-tinged peanut halves. A pair of them sit facing each other inside the fruit, although 5 to 10 percent of the time a single bean, called a peaberry, is found.

- coffee bean
- mucilage
- silver skin
- parchment
- pulp

211

After Coffee

ACROSS

1 Frequently, in poems
4 Ticket add-on
7 Qty.
10 Kanga's son
11 *Oedipus* ___
12 Animal house?
13 **Frosted treat**
15 "So that's it!"
16 Light crime?
17 Caramel-colored drinks
19 Nipper's co.
21 Eye of ___
22 **Trains, as a puppy**
26 As to
27 Divinity sch.
28 Iowa or Ohio
30 Use a tub
34 Moral wrong
35 **Tossed item**
37 Bird on the Australian coat of arms
38 Choose
39 Mo. with no national holidays
40 ___ Moines, Iowa
41 Scot's "no"
42 Literary monogram

DOWN

1 Killer whale
2 A quartet
3 Outdoes
4 Gustave Eiffel's country of birth
5 Comics cry
6 Co. bigwig
7 Flowering shrub
8 Hairdo with shaved sides
9 Raised-glass speeches
14 Item cinched around the waist
18 Small type of band
20 Crunch targets, for short
22 Made snake sounds
23 Not late
24 Seventh planet from the Sun
25 Money back offer
29 Poet's "black"
31 Ski lift type
32 Drag
33 Dairy dozen
36 Clean air org.

1 2 3 4 5 6 7 8 9
10 11 12
13 14 15
16 17 18
19 20 21
22 23 24 25
26 27
28 29 30 31 32 33
34 35 36
37 38 39
40 41 42

After Coffee

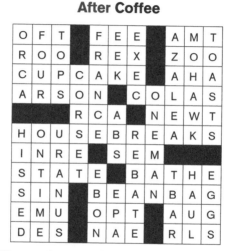

O	F	T		F	E	E		A	M	T
R	O	O		R	E	X		Z	O	O
C	U	P	C	A	K	E		A	H	A
A	R	S	O	N		C	O	L	A	S
		R	C	A		N	E	W	T
H	O	U	S	E	B	R	E	A	K	S
I	N	R	E		S	E	M			
S	T	A	T	E		B	A	T	H	E
S	I	N		B	E	A	N	B	A	G
E	M	U		O	P	T		A	U	G
D	E	S		N	A	E		R	L	S

The words cup, cake, house, breaks, bean,
and bag can all follow the word coffee

214

With European ports unable to receive coffee shipments during World War II, the United States became the sole market for Latin and South American beans. After D-Day, while Europeans faced scarcities and exorbitant prices, American troops had a nearly limitless supply.

Marat, Robespierre, Danton, and other French Revolutionaries did much of their plotting in Paris's Café de Procope coffeehouse, often while a young artillery officer by the name of Napoleon Bonaparte played chess at a nearby table.

I would rather suffer with coffee than be senseless.

. . .

NAPOLEON BONAPARTE (1769–1821)

EXCERPTS FROM A 1674 LONDON BROADSIDE

Above: Woodcut illustration from the broadside

First sent amongst us the *All-healing-Berry*
At once to make us both *Sober* and *Merry*.
Arabian Coffee, a Rich Cordial
To Purse and Person Beneficial...

Do but this Rare ARABIAN Cordial use,
And thou may'st all the Doctors Slops Refuse.
Hush then, dull QUACKS, your Mountebanking
  cease,
COFFEE's a speedier Cure for each Disease.
How great its Vertues are, we hence may think,
The Worlds third Part makes it their common
  Drink;
In Breif (sic), all you who Healths Rich Treasures
  Prize,
And Court not Ruby Noses, or blear'd Eyes,
But own Sobriety to be your Drift,
And Love at once good Company and Thrift;
To Wine no more make Wit and Coyn a Trophy,
But come each Night and Frollique here in
  Coffee.

Career Path

The British sitcom *As Time Goes By* chronicled the lives of Lionel and Jean, young lovers who lost touch in 1953 only to meet again 38 years later. Find the sitcom-related words in the grid and then read the leftover letters to find Lionel's occupation while he and Jean were apart.

AGENCY	JUDITH	PENNY
ALISTAIR	KOREA	POOH
ARMY	LIONEL	ROCKY
HARDCASTLE	MADGE	SANDY
HARRY	NURSE	STEPHEN
JEAN	MRS. BALE	

```
H  E  M  R  J  E  A  N  Y  A
H  A  R  R  Y  U  N  A  M  S
A  C  O  N  S  F  D  F  R  T
R  E  L  U  E  B  P  I  A  E
D  A  E  R  O  K  A  L  T  P
C  A  N  S  N  T  T  L  P  H
A  E  O  E  S  A  T  O  E  E
S  G  I  I  I  A  O  O  N  N
T  D  L  N  I  H  N  N  N  K
L  A  G  E  N  C  Y  D  Y  E
E  M  N  Y  R  O  C  K  Y  A
```

Career Path

```
H  E  M  R  J  E  A  N  Y  A
H  A  R  R  Y  U  N  A  M  S
A  C  O  N  S  F  D  F  R  T
R  E  L  U  E  B  P  I  A  E
D  A  E  R  O  K  A  L  T  P
C  A  N  S  N  T  T  L  P  H
A  E  O  E  S  A  T  O  E  E
S  G  I  I  I  A  O  O  N  N
T  D  L  N  I  H  N  N  N  K
L  A  G  E  N  C  Y  D  Y  E
E  M  N  Y  R  O  C  K  Y  A
```

HE RAN A COFFEE
PLANTATION IN KENYA

Prior to coffee's introduction, 17th century Germans often drank flour soup and beer for breakfast.

The coffee plant's white flowers look like orange blossoms, smell of jasmine, and last but a few days.

*Free yourselves
from the slavery
of tea and coffee and
other slop-kettle.*

• • •

WILLIAM COBBETT
social reformer and proponent of rural values
Advice to Young Men (1929)

The Four S's

The true art of coffee tasting, a precise process requiring skill and an experienced palate, is practiced by fewer than 50 professionals in the United States. Pans filled with green and roasted beans are examined and then the cup-tasting, or cupping, begins.

1. SMELL: Water just off the boil is poured into a white, 6 oz. china cup containing two tablespoons of freshly ground coffee. The grounds form a crust on top of the water, which is inhaled deeply. The crust is broken with a silver spoon and a second inhalation is taken.

2. SLURP: After removing any residue from the top of the cup, the taster takes a spoonful of coffee and *violently* slurps it, spraying it over the tongue. This aerates the coffee and prevents it from mixing with the saliva.

3. SWISH: The coffee is rolled about the mouth to all parts of the tongue.

4. SPIT: When the taster is done, the sample is unceremoniously spit into a small, metal receptacle known as a garboon.

New York Coffee Exchange graders, early 1900s

Brewdoku

These nine letters fill the grid:

CATSUP NOW

Each letter must appear once in each row, once in each column, and once in every 3x3 square.

The highlighted letters answer this clue:

**What some find preferable
to a cup of coffee**

		C		A		S		
A						U		O
U			P		C			N
	T		A		W		U	
		U				W		
	C		T		N		P	
O			U		T			W
C		T						A
		S		N		T		

Brewdoku

T	N	C	O	A	U	S	W	P
A	P	W	N	T	S	U	C	O
U	S	O	P	W	C	A	T	N
S	T	P	A	O	W	N	U	C
N	O	U	S	C	P	W	A	T
W	C	A	T	U	N	O	P	S
O	A	N	U	P	T	C	S	W
C	U	T	W	S	O	P	N	A
P	W	S	C	N	A	T	O	U

TWO CUPS

Coffee-drinking Americans consume an average of just over three cups a day. That adds up to about 150 billion cups per year.

This coffee falls into your stomach, and straightway there is a general commotion. Ideas begin to move like the battalions of the Grand Army on the battlefield, and the battle takes place. Things remembered arrive at full gallop, ensign to the wind. The light cavalry of comparisons deliver a magnificent deploying charge, the artillery of logic hurry up with their train and ammunition, the shafts of wit start

up like sharpshooters. *Similes arise,*
the paper is covered with ink; for
the struggle commences and is con-
cluded with torrents of black water,
just as a battle with powder.

...

HONORÉ DE BALZAC (1773)

*Coffee makes
us severe, and grave,
and philosophical.*

...

JONATHAN SWIFT (1722)

Daniel Webster described the Green Dragon coffeehouse and tavern as "the headquarters of the Revolution." It was there that unhappy patriots brewed up the Boston Tea Party.

Cream and Sugar

All the words in the list are made from
the letters in CREAM AND SUGAR.
Place each one into the grid.

3 letters:

ARM   SUM
NAG   SUN
SEA

4 letters:

DARE   READ
ECRU   REAM
GAME   SANG

5 letters:

ARENA
DUNES
NEARS
NUDGE
RACER

6 letters:

AGENDA
AMUSED
DANGER
DREAMS
RAGMAN

7 letters:

ARRANGE
EARDRUM
REGARDS

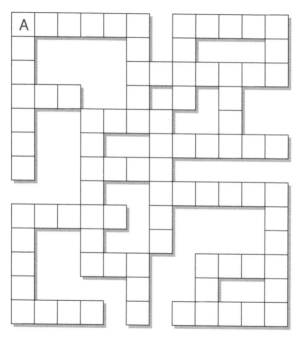

237

Cream and Sugar

Paris became one vast café.
Conversation in France was at its
zenith...The intangible flow of wit
was as spontaneous as possible.
For this sparkling outburst there
is no doubt that honor should be
ascribed in part to...the great event
which created new customs, and
even modified human temperament
—the advent of coffee.

...

JULES MICHELET, French historian (1798–1874)
describing 18th century Paris

King Gustav III of Sweden once commuted a pair of twin's death sentences to life in prison with the stipulation that one of them was to be served a large bowl of tea three times a day, the other coffee, to determine the healthier beverage. Tea lost. The twin who drank it died first at the age of 83, a few years before his brother.

*Life is just
one cup of coffee
after another, and
don't look for
anything else.*

. . .

Said to be the last words of
BERTRAND RUSSELL (1872)

Strong
enough
to float a
horseshoe

...

OLD WEST DESCRIPTION
OF THE PERFECT
CUP OF COFFEE

Here lies cut down like an unripe fruit,
The wife of Deacon Amos Shute:
She died of drinking too much coffee,
Anny Dominy eighteen forty.

• • •

FREDERIC W. UNGER, *Epitaphs* (1905)
from a tombstone in Connecticut

16 Cups of COFFEE

The word COFFEE appears 16 times in this grid. Look for it reading left, right, up, down, and diagonally in all directions.

```
C  C  O  F  F  E  E  C  C  E
C  O  F  F  E  E  E  F  F  O  C
O  C  F  F  F  E  E  E  E  O  F
F  C  O  F  F  E  E  F  E  O  F
F  C  O  F  E  F  C  F  F  C  O
E  C  O  F  F  E  E  F  F  O  C
E  C  C  O  F  F  E  E  O  O  C
C  O  C  E  E  F  F  O  C  O  C
```

32 Cups of JAVA

The word JAVA appears 32 times in this grid. Look for it reading left, right, up, down, and diagonally in all directions.

```
J  A  V  A  J  A  V  A  J  A  J
A  A  A  J  A  V  A  J  A  V  A
V  V  V  V  V  A  J  A  V  A  V
A  J  A  A  A  A  J  A  A  J  A
A  V  A  J  J  J  V  A  V  A  J
A  J  A  A  A  A  A  J  A  A  A
A  V  V  V  J  A  V  V  V  A  V
A  A  A  A  J  A  V  A  A  J  A
```

ANSWER

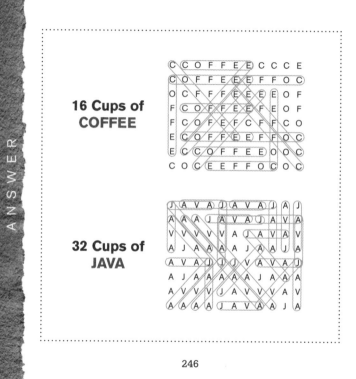

16 Cups of COFFEE

32 Cups of JAVA

*Coffee is balm
to the heart and
spirit.*

...

GIUSEPPE VERDI
(1820–1869)

Coffee & Health

While drinking too much coffee can have undesirable consequences, including insomnia and excessive urination, scientific studies have shown moderate caffeine consumption to have a number of *positive* health benefits.

Antioxidants: Coffee (regular, decaf, or instant) contains four times the antioxidants of green tea.

Enhanced Performance: Coffee can improve performance in tests of reaction time, memory, and spatial reasoning. Athletic performance and recovery time have also been shown to benefit from caffeine intake.

Reduced Risk: Research indicates that moderate caffeine consumption can alleviate asthma symptoms in some people, decrease the risk of contracting type-2 diabetes, and reduce the odds of developing Parkinson's Disease (in men, at least) and Alzheimer's. It also can lessen the likelihood of both kidney stone and gallstone production and has been shown to significantly lower the chances of developing colorectal cancer.

And More: Studies have found coffee can fight an array of bacteria, including one that causes tooth decay. It can also lessen headaches, suicidal feelings, depression, and irritability, so go ahead, drink up. Coffee may be doing more than keeping you awake.

Coffee isn't my cup of tea.
...

SAMUEL GOLDWYN (1879–1974)

Qahwa,
the Arabic word
for coffee from
which the English
word derives, was
originally a poetic
term for wine.

Split Personalities

On the next page, rearrange the two-letter pieces to form an author's name. Enter one letter per space keeping the new order.

Then take the numbered letters only and transfer them to the same-numbered blanks below to name the author of this 1802 quote:

The principle coffeehouses here [Paris] are fitted up with taste and elegance. Large mirrors form no inconsiderable part of their decoration. There are no partitions to divide them into boxes. The tables are of marble; the benches and stools are covered with Utrecht velvet.

<u>   </u> <u>   </u> <u>   </u> <u>   </u> <u>   </u> <u>   </u> <u>   </u>   <u>   </u>
 1   2   3   4   5   6   7   8

<u>   </u> <u>   </u> <u>   </u> <u>   </u> <u>   </u> <u>   </u> <u>   </u>
 9 10 11 12 13 14 15

1. GE   GE   LL   OR   OR   WE

_ _ _ _ _ _   _ _ _ _
12   8

2. AF   AN   FR   KA   ZK

_ _ _ _ _   _ _ _ _ _
1   15   11

3. AU   EN   JA   NE   ST

_ _ _ _   _ _ _ _ _
3   7

4. DO   ES   NG   RI   SI   SL

_ _ _ _ _   _ _ _ _ _ _ _
13 14   6

5. AR   CH   IC   KE   LE   NS   SD

_ _ _ _ _ _   _ _ _ _ _ _
10   5   4

6. AM   BR   ER   OK   ST

_ _ _ _   _ _ _ _ _ _
9   2

253

Split Personalities

1. GEORGE ORWELL
2. FRANZ KAFKA
3. JANE AUSTEN
4. DORIS LESSING
5. CHARLES DICKENS
6. BRAM STOKER

FRANCIS W. BLAGDON

Quote from *Paris As It Was and As It Is*
(a series of letters written to a friend in London
while traveling during the years 1801–02)

I'm
nothing
before
my
morning
coffee.

The world downs over one
billion cups of coffee every day.

That's just over a sixth of a cup of
coffee for every person on the planet.

*Behind every
successful woman...
is a substantial
amount of coffee.*

. . .

STEPHANIE PIRO (1996)

I think if
I were a woman
I'd wear coffee
as a perfume.

...

JOHN VAN DRUTEN
(1901–1975)

Agatha Christie's first stage play was titled *Black Coffee*. It featured Hercule Poirot and debuted in London's Embassy Theatre in 1930 to decent reviews.

Bean
Maze #3

Move diagonally from
roasted bean to roasted
bean one bean at a time.
You can also jump over
an unroasted bean, but
only if there's a roast-
ed bean on the
other side.

START

END

261

PUZZLE

Bean Maze #3

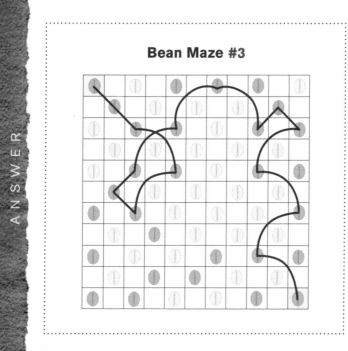

Three longtime
fixtures on Johnny
Carson's *Tonight Show*
desk were his lighter, a
wooden cigarette box, and
a coffee mug with an oval
picture of himself on it.

Arabica

Coffea arabica

- Discovered in Ethiopia approximately 500–600 A.D.
- The world's premium coffee and the most widely grown species, accounting for about 70 percent of all coffee
- Thrives in sunny, tropical settings at altitudes between 3,000 and 6,500 feet
- Doesn't like extreme heat or cold

Robusta

Coffea canephora

- Discovered in the Belgian Congo in 1898
- Cheaper to grow but produces a weaker, more bitter cupful; accounts for nearly 30 percent of all coffee
- A hardier and higher-yielding plant that does well at lower altitudes
- Contains about one and a half times as much caffeine as arabica

By the King.

A PROCLAMATION

FOR THE

Suppression of Coffee-Houses.

In 1675, King Charles II of England imposed a ban on coffeehouses that never came to pass. Public opposition forced him to recall it two days before it took effect. At right is an excerpt from it.

...the multitude of Coffee-Houses...have produced very evil and dangerous effects... in such houses divers false, malitious and scandalous reports are devised and spread abroad to the Defamation of his Majestie's Government, and to the Disturbance of the Peace and Quiet of the Realm...

Happy Hour

In 2007, researchers at the University of Cambridge found that workers are happier and more productive when companies...

To finish this thought, find and circle each occupation, then read the leftover letters. (And then send a memo to your boss.)

ACTUARY	DANCER	PAVER
ACTOR	DOCTOR	PILOT
ASTRONOMER	JUDGE	PORTER
ATTORNEY	MASON	PRINTER
AUTHOR	MODEL	TAILOR
BUTCHER	NANNY	TUTOR
COMPOSER	PAINTER	WAITER
COOK		

```
A  S  T  R  O  N  O  M  E  R  L  E
U  T  T  E  M  P  A  V  E  R  K  A
T  P  T  R  O  L  I  A  T  O  L  C
H  R  M  O  D  E  L  L  O  O  R  T
O  P  E  Y  R  O  T  C  O  D  E  U
R  E  O  S  E  N  R  S  A  T  H  A
E  S  O  R  O  E  E  N  C  I  C  R
T  J  A  L  T  P  C  Y  R  I  T  Y
N  Z  U  I  E  E  M  O  O  U  U  N
I  V  A  D  R  E  R  O  T  R  B  N
R  W  C  O  G  F  F  O  C  E  E  A
P  A  I  N  T  E  R  M  A  S  O  N
```

PUZZLE

Happy Hour

...LET EMPLOYEES
SOCIALIZE OVER COFFEE

The coffee crop is so vital to Colombia's economy that every vehicle entering the country is sprayed for bacteria that would harm the crop.

"Percolator," a pop song that used a Moog synthesizer to imitate the sound of percolating coffee, debuted in 1973. It flopped.

The coffee is prepared in such a way that it makes those who drink it witty: at least there is not a single soul who, on quitting the house, does not believe himself four times wittier that when he entered it.

. . .

CHARLES-LOUIS DE SECONDAT
(1689–1755)

*If this is coffee,
please bring me some
tea; but if this is
tea, please bring
me some coffee.*

...

ABRAHAM LINCOLN (1809–1865)

A contestant on Bravo's *Project Runway* once made a dress entirely out of coffee filters. The challenge was to design a garment using only materials found in the contestants' apartments. Alas, the frilly filter design lost out to a tailored blue bed sheet.

Do-It-Yourself Crossword

We removed 10 letters from this mini-crossword and listed them at the top of the next page. We've also included the list of clues needed for it. Your job is to put the letters back in the grid and figure out which clue goes with which Across or Down number.

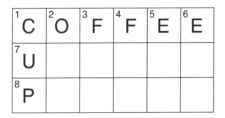

Letters to put in the grid:

A C E E L N N O T Y

Clues:

ACROSS

1 Joe

7 ___

8 ___

DOWN

1 Joe holder

2 ___

3 ___

4 ___

5 ___

6 ___

A. System prefix

B. Dusk, to poets

C. Buzzing pest

D. Loosen, as shoes

E. Place of fiction

F. Whole milk ingredient

G. It's said before "blastoff"

PUZZLE

Do-It-Yourself Crossword

C	O	F	F	E	E
U	N	L	A	C	E
P	E	Y	T	O	N

ACROSS:

1. Joe
7. D Loosen, as shoes
8. E Place of fiction

DOWN:

1. Joe holder
2. G It's said before "blastoff"
3. C Buzzing pest
4. F Whole milk ingredient
5. A System prefix
6. B Dusk, to poets

ANSWER

278

Black coffee is never served at a fashionable dinner table, but is brought afterwards with cigarettes and liqueurs into the drawing-room for the ladies, and with cigars, cigarettes and liqueurs into the smoking room for the gentlemen.

. . .

EMILY POST, *Etiquette* (1922)

The #1 reason
men drink coffee:
to get work done

The #1 reason
women drink coffee:
to relax

I have measured out my life with coffee spoons.

. . .

T. S. ELIOT

"The Love Song of J. Alfred Prufrock" (1917)

For over a century all coffee exports came from Arabia Felix (Yemen). The monopoly was broken in the 1600s when a man named Baba Budan managed to smuggle out seven live beans to India.

Offspring from those seven beans, called "Old Chik," account for about one-third of the coffee grown in India today.

Doctor's Orders

Fill in the eight answers on the next page.
Then transfer the letters to the same-
numbered spaces below to find out
what the doctor told the coffee drinker.

$\overline{}$ $\overline{1}$ $\overline{2}$ $\overline{3}$ $\overline{4}$ $\overline{5}$ $\overline{6}$ $\overline{7}$

$\overline{8}$ $\overline{9}$ $\overline{10}$ $\overline{11}$ $\overline{12}$ $\overline{13}$ $\overline{14}$

$\overline{15}$ $\overline{16}$ $\overline{17}$ $\overline{18}$ $\overline{19}$ $\overline{20}$ $\overline{21}$ $\overline{22}$

$\overline{23}$ $\overline{24}$ $\overline{25}$ $\overline{26}$ $\overline{27}$ $\overline{28}$ $\overline{29}$ $\overline{30}$ $\overline{31}$

$\overline{32}$ $\overline{33}$ $\overline{34}$ $\overline{35}$ $\overline{36}$ $\overline{37}$ $\overline{38}$ $\overline{39}$ $\overline{40}$ $\overline{41}$.

1. Gave out cards ___ ___ ___ ___ ___
14   4   16   30   41

2. Spirit ___ ___ ___ ___ ___
39   24   7   11   34

3. Swindled ___ ___ ___ ___ ___ ___ ___
8   40   20   12   1   31   28

4. Type of can or ear ___ ___ ___
23   38   22

5. Paired, as socks ___ ___ ___ ___ ___
19   2   5   25   29

6. Lecherous guy ___ ___ ___ ___
6   32   17   33

7. Oz resident ___ ___ ___ ___ ___ ___ ___ ___
26   9   13   15   35   3   27   37

8. Heap ___ ___ ___ ___
10   21   18   36

Doctor's Orders

1. DEALT
2. GHOST
3. CHEATED
4. TIN
5. MATED
6. WOLF
7. MUNCHKIN
8. PILE

TAKE TWO CUPS AND CALL ME IN
THE MIDDLE OF THE NIGHT

Coffee is a most powerful antiseptic, and therefore very useful as a disinfectant. It has been used as a specific against cholera with marvellous results, and is useful in all cases of intestinal derangement...I do not recommend coffee as a beverage, but as a medicine.

. . .

FLORENCE DANIEL
Food Remedies (1908)

*Coffee is a
beverage that
puts one to sleep
when not drunk.*

• • •

ALPHONSE ALLAIS
French writer and humorist (1854–1905)

Coffee Cantata

In 1732, Johann Sebastian Bach turned a humorous poem by Picander into what's become known as the *Coffee Cantata*. It's original title was "Be Quiet, Don't Chatter."

Ah! Coffee, how lovely this is,
Sweeter than a thousand kisses,
Mellower than muscatel.
Coffee, coffee, I crave it dearly;
And should someone wish to cheer me,
Take my cup and fill it well!

Although often thought of as a tea-drinking nation, Japan is the third largest consumer of coffee in the world.

It fortifies the members, it cleans the skin, and dries up the humidities that are under it and gives an excellent smell to all the body.

...

AVICENNA (c. 1000 A.D.)
Persian philosopher and scientist

Brewdoku

These nine letters fill the grid:

TINSEL BAR

Each letter must appear once in each row, once in each column, and once in every 3x3 square.

The highlighted letters answer this clue:

They're used for making coffee...
or solving puzzles

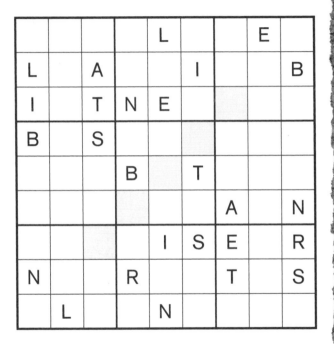

				L			E	
L		A			I			B
I		T	N	E				
B		S						
			B		T			
						A		N
				I	S	E		R
N			R			T		S
	L			N				

PUZZLE

Brewdoku

R	S	N	A	L	B	I	E	T
L	E	A	S	T	I	N	R	B
I	B	T	N	E	R	S	A	L
B	A	S	I	R	N	L	T	E
E	N	L	B	A	T	R	S	I
T	R	I	E	S	L	A	B	N
A	T	B	L	I	S	E	N	R
N	I	E	R	B	A	T	L	S
S	L	R	T	N	E	B	I	A

BEANS

One 1980s Tokyo spa offered a coffee bath in which patrons could soak their cares away in a pool of soggy, ground, and fermented coffee. The mixture, kept at a toasty 140°F, was touted as being no less than "the solution of all diseases."

What other drink has a table named after it . . . even if it's only used to hold our rarely read coffee-table books?

One cup of coffee is worth forty years of friendship.

...

OLD TURKISH SAYING

*A mathematician is
a machine for turning
coffee into theorems.*

...

PAUL ERDÖS
Hungarian mathematician (1913–1996)

In Stalag Luft III, site of the famed "Great Escape," Red Cross packages provided Allied prisoners with American coffee, for bribing the guards, and Klim (milk spelled backwards) tins, which were fit together to make ventilation tubes for their escape tunnels.

Olde Riddle

Fill each rectangle with two or three letters
to make words reading both across and
down. The filled-in letters, from 1 to 11, will
answer this riddle from an 1859 book:

Why is coffee like an
axe with a dull edge?

```
          WA                        ISTH
1   SU  [      ]  ABLE     2    A  [      ]  EMENT
          RESS                       ES


          MEA                         D
3   OU  [      ]  ACK      4   TEL  [      ]  AM
          ALL                        EE
```

5 M [AST / D] TAIN   6 HAN [SAN / OX] ALL

7 PR [R / UND] ACE   8 T [F / CAST] ADOR

9 C [IN / AL] ZEN   10 CAP [RE / ME] LE

11 NO [SUPPO / LY] IVE

_____

_____

_____

Olde Riddle

1 IT   WAITRESS-SUITABLE
2 MUS ISTHMUSES-AMUSEMENT
3 TB   MEATBALL-OUTBACK
4 EGR DEGREE-TELEGRAM
5 OUN ASTOUND-MOUNTAIN
6 DB   SANDBOX-HANDBALL
7 EF   REFUND-PREFACE
8 ORE FORECAST-TOREADOR
9 ITI INITIAL-CITIZEN
10 SU   RESUME-CAPSULE
11 SED SUPPOSEDLY-NOSEDIVE

IT MUST BE GROUND
BEFORE IT IS USED

All fathers and mothers should make their children abstain from coffee, if they do not wish them at twenty to be puny dried-up machines.

...

JEAN-ANTHELME BRILLAT-SAVARIN

The Physiology of Taste (1825)

Early Coffee

The first use of coffee wasn't as a drink but as an energy food. In the 7th century, the nomadic Oromo people of Ethiopia mixed fat with crushed coffee and molded it into golfball-sized snacks.

Kati, a brew made from steeping roasted coffee leaves in hot water, and *kisher*, a straw-colored drink made from roasted coffee husks, also predate the use of roasted coffee beans to make the beverage. Kati and kisher are still drunk today on the Arabian peninsula and in Ethiopia.

I wish you were the coffee cup,
  From which I drink my brew.
For then I know at every sup,
  A kiss I'd give to you.

Gas coffee roaster, 1891

Coffee is so complex that scientists haven't been able to chemically analyze all the processes that take place during roasting.

In Europe, coffee is an unknown beverage. You can get what the European hotel-keeper thinks is coffee, but it resembles the real thing as hypocrisy resembles holiness.

...

MARK TWAIN
A Tramp Abroad (1880)

Coffee Celebrities

ACROSS

1 C-shaped tool
6 Upright part of a stairway
11 Out of port
12 Cutting edge
13 **Coffee-making actor?**
15 Atl. crosser, once
16 Profs' aides
17 Meteor end
18 Neg. opposite
19 The Bard's river
20 **Coffee-serving almanac author?**
24 ___ account (never)
25 Gun owners' org.
26 28-Across's charge
27 Greek vowel
28 NCO
31 **Seconds-dispensing host?**
34 Pimento's nest
35 Prepared to be dubbed
36 Fasten again
37 Dog cries

DOWN

1 Taxis
2 Env. innards
3 "I'd hate to break up ___"
4 Kitten's cry
5 Minister
6 Stat for a slugger
7 Sick
8 Mouth moisture
9 Manuscript checker
10 E-mail again
14 Really got involved with
18 Not con
19 "Eureka!"
20 Take care of, as expenses
21 Catalogued
22 Detach, from a leash
23 Grouchy
27 Adam's birthplace
28 Poet/author Silverstein
29 Chug
30 Vietnam holidays
32 VIII x VII
33 Meth- or eth- suffix

PUZZLE

Coffee Celebrities

C	L	A	M	P		R	I	S	E	R
A	T	S	E	A		B	L	A	D	E
B	R	E	W	S	W	I	L	L	I	S
S	S	T		T	A	S		I	T	E
		P	O	S		A	V	O	N	
P	O	U	R	R	I	C	H	A	R	D
O	N	N	O		N	R	A			
P	F	C		E	T	A		S	G	T
F	I	L	L	D	O	N	A	H	U	E
O	L	I	V	E		K	N	E	L	T
R	E	P	I	N		Y	E	L	P	S

310

The first coffee drunk
in space was in 1968
by the Apollo 7 crew.

Otto von Bismarck, first chancellor of the German Empire (1815–1898), was in a country inn in France one day and asked the host if there was any chicory in the house. Told there was, he asked for it all to be brought to him. Several containers were hauled out to his

table, and after being assured that was the inn's total supply, Bismarck said, "Good, now go and make me a pot of coffee."

NEWS from the COFFE-HOUSE;

In which is shewn their several sorts of Passions,
Containing Newes from all our Neighbour *Nations*.

A POEM.

There's nothing done in all the World,
    From Monarch to the Mouse
But every Day or Night 'tis hurld
    Into the Coffee-house.
What Lillie or what Booker can*
    By Art, not bring about,
At Coffee-house you'll find a Man,
    Can quickly find it out.

• • •

FROM A LONDON COFFEEHOUSE BROADSIDE (1667)

*Lillie was an astrologer and Booker a prognosticator

Lloyd's of London

began as Lloyd's, a 17th century
London coffeehouse where seafarers
and marine-insurance brokers met
to conduct their business.

ON THIS SITE BETWEEN 1680 AND 1778 STOOD JONATHAN'S COFFEE HOUSE, THE PRINCIPAL MEETING PLACE OF THE CITY'S STOCKBROKERS

The London Stock Exchange

traces its origins back to Jonathan's coffeehouse, not far from Lloyd's. Until recently, its messengers were called waiters, a holdover from early days.

Coffeepot give us peace
coffeepot let children grow
let our wealth swell
please protect us from evils.

. . .

ANCIENT ETHIOPIAN PRAYER

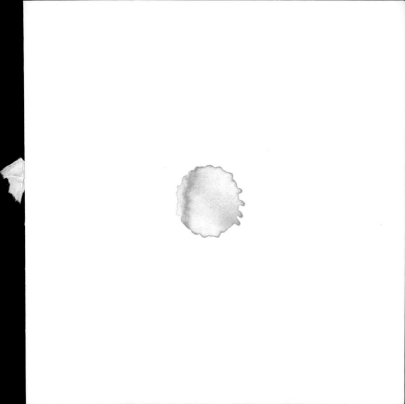

Credits & Sources

10   Courtesy of NASA TV

11, 144, 256, 311 Photos courtesy of NASA

19   ©1937, 1938 by Random House, Inc.,
        renewed 1965 by Rungstedlundfonden

59   Photos courtesy of Wayne Donohue

64, 299 Personal collection of Patrick Merrell

74, 128 Sutphen, *Uncensored Situations*

81   Jean-Baptiste van Mour (1720)

82   Permission of Dr. Quentin Stafford-Fraser

87, 147 Sears, Roebuck Catalogue (1902 edition)

97, 289 Translations by Patrick Merrell

114   Background courtesy mipolonia.net

122   *Tea & Coffee Trade Journal,* Feb. 1920

161   Ambigram ©2007 Patrick Merrell

192   Library of Congress (1905)

194–195 Gillette, *The White House Cookbook* (1887)

202   Source: Center for Science in the Public Interest

258   Permission of Stephanie Piro, *Caffeinated Cartoons*

Ukers, *All About Coffee*: 1, 2, 18, 24, 32, 33, 47, 57, 73, 98, 100, 104, 105, 151, 153, 154, 155, 170, 200, 207, 208, 218, 224, 227, 235, 266, 306, 314, 319, 320

Antique illustrations: Dover Publications: Harter, *Animals*; Harter, *Harter's Picture Archive*; Harter, *Food and Drink*; Gillon, *Picture Sourcebook for Collage*; Grafton, *Humorous Victorian Spot Illustrations* Additional antique illustrations: *Desk Gallery* images by permission of clipart.com

Helene's puzzles (every other puzzle):
12, 28, 44, 60, 76, 92, 108, 124, 140,
156, 172, 188, 204, 220, 236, 252,
268, 284, 300
Patrick's puzzles: 20, (29), 36, 52,
68, 84, 100, 116, 132, 148, 164,
180, 196, 212, 228, 244, 260,
276, 292, 308

Patrick Merrell drinks his coffee black, in the morning and after bicycle races. He's a writer, graphic designer, illustrator, cartoonist, and puzzlemaker (including crossword puzzles for *The New York Times*) and lives in Mount Vernon, NY, with his wife and daughter.

Helene Hovanec drinks many mugs of coffee (with cream) all morning long. She's the author of numerous puzzle books and is very involved in the puzzle world, most notably with the American Crossword Puzzle Tournament and the World Puzzle Championship. She lives in Brooklyn, NY.